# AFFY AND MILO

ESTER LÓPEZ

Illustrated by
KIERSTON DUNFEE

Persephone Press

COVER DESIGN and ILLUSTRATIONS
by
Kierston Dunfee

Hardback
ISBN: 979-8-9884483-6-5

Paperback
ISBN: 979-8-9884483-7-2

*For my granddaughters and all those who love Pekin Ducks*

# 1

## AFFY

Once upon a time, there was a little Pekin Duck named Affy.

Affy shared a coop with some chickens, and they lived along the French Broad River. Pekin ducks can live to be up to twelve years, which is very old for a duck.

*Affy*

*Affy and the chickens*

# 2

## AFFY AND CHICKENS

Each day, Affy would join the chickens and scavenge for earthworms, newts, dandelions, clover, crickets and marigolds. Affy also liked lettuce and wild strawberries.

*Affy eating strawberries*

*Affy and the chickens in the coop*

# 3

## OTHER CRITTERS

Pekin ducks have no way to protect themselves from other animals that might want to hurt them. So at night, to be safe from predators, Affy and the chickens slept in the chicken coop. They would eat feed with corn and protein. Some of the predators along the river were hawks, minks, raccoons, and owls, but there were more predators away from the river.

*Predators*

# 4

## MILO

Affy was quiet and calm but couldn't fly. He had a curl at the end of his tail, called a drake feather. He was a happy little duck.

One day, a mallard duck landed in the yard. Mallards can fly. This little duck was called Milo.

*Milo*

# 5

## AFFY AND MILO

Milo showed Affy how to forage for fish, frogs, and algae in the river. Affy and Milo swam around the dock. Some nights, the two stayed in the river all night and were safe from the land critters.

During the day, Affy and Milo hung out with the chickens in the yard. Affy enjoyed Milo's company.

# 6

## DAISY

One day, another Pekin duck was introduced to Affy. Her name was Daisy. Daisy was a very small duck. Daisy stayed with Affy and the chickens in the coop at night, while Milo swam in the river.

When Daisy got bigger, she quacked loudly. Affy's quack was soft. Milo and Affy showed Daisy how to catch fish in the river and how to stay safe at night.

One day, Daisy laid an egg on the dock. She quacked a lot to let everyone know her good news. Did you know female Pekin ducks can lay up to 150 eggs per year? The eggs are good to eat and much bigger than chicken eggs. We gathered up the duck eggs, along with the chicken eggs for eating.

Daisy continued to forage for food in the yard with Affy and Milo during the day. Then at night, Daisy and Affy swam around in the river to keep Milo company. Milo would not go into the chicken coop.

# 7

## MILO

Then, one day, Milo flew away. Affy and Daisy looked all around the yard for Milo but they couldn't find him. They hung out with the chickens during the day. That night, Affy and Daisy stayed in the coop with the chickens.

One night, Affy and Daisy wouldn't go into the coop with the chickens. They stayed in the water all night.

# 8

## GOODBYE

T he next day, Affy and Daisy swam down the river to start a
life of their own.

*Affy and Milo down by the river*

*Milo and Affy heading to the river for a swim*

*Affy and Daisy going for a swim after Milo left*

# ADVENTURE STREET KIDS

The next book in my children's books will be for grades 3 up to 6. Join a group of kids living on Adventure Street as they try to solve a crime.

# ABOUT THE AUTHOR

Ester López is a sci-fi and paranormal adventure writer and screenwriter, writing on the edge of reality. This is her fourth children's book, which is a non-fiction story told in a fictional way. She lives in the Smoky Mountain area with her husband, new puppy, Chewie, and two mini horses, Pepper and Bucky.

You can find Ester's other books on her website at:
www.writingphotographicservicesllc.com
If you like the story, please give it an honest review at your favorite retailer.

facebook.com/EsterLopezAuthor
twitter.com/esterlopez1
instagram.com/esterlopez2956

www.ingramcontent.com/pod-product-compliance
Lightning Source LLC
Chambersburg PA
CBHW041935260326
41914CB00010B/1305